Learn About

YOUR B

I Can Be a
Good
Friend

written by Meredith Rusu

illustrated by Alexandra Colombo

Children's Press®
An imprint of Scholastic Inc.

Special thanks to Doctor Ann (Nancy) Close, Assistant Professor of the Yale School of Medicine and member of the Child Study Center at Yale University, for her insight into the development of children in early childhood.

Library of Congress Cataloging-in-Publication Data available
ISBN 978-1-339-02063-1 (library binding) | ISBN 978-1-339-02064-8 (paperback)

10 9 8 7 6 5 4 3 2 1   24 25 26 27 28

Printed in China, 62
First edition, 2024

Book design by Kathleen Petelinsek

TABLE OF CONTENTS

I Can Be a Good Friend

Hi! My name is Hikaru. Today, our class is going to the zoo!

We each have a buddy. My buddy is Nihal. He has a broken leg, so it's my job to help him.

Our teacher asked us to practice being good friends today because that's how **FRIENDSHIP GROWS**.

I wonder if she's right?

I can be a good friend by **sharing** my seat.

Nihal has his crutches. I don't mind squishing a little so we can sit together.

FRIENDSHIP GROWS!

Nihal teaches me a clapping game.

I can be a good friend by being **patient** as Nihal gets off the bus.

I know he needs a little extra time.

ZOO MAP

FRIENDSHIP GROWS!
Nihal grabs an extra zoo map so we each have our own.

I can be a good friend by working together with Nihal to find our favorite animals at the zoo. Mine are the tigers. His are the red pandas.

FRIENDSHIP GROWS!

Nihal says, "Let's go see the tigers first!"

RED PANDA

I can be a good friend by helping Nihal complete his checklist for our zoo project.

It's tricky for him to write while he's holding on to his crutches.

FRIENDSHIP GROWS!

Nihal points out some cool red panda facts!

TIGER

RED PANDA

ELEPHANT

I can be a good friend by sitting with Nihal at lunch, even though some other kids ask me to sit with them.

I **promised** Nihal that we would eat together.

FRIENDSHIP GROWS!

We all decide to sit as one big group instead!

I can be a good friend by keeping Nihal company since he can't play on the playground. We'll definitely do the monkey bars once his leg is healed.

FRIENDSHIP GROWS!

We discover a butterfly garden, and I show Nihal how to get a butterfly to land on his finger!

Secret Butterfly Garden

I can be a good friend by not teasing a classmate when she cries.

Nihal thinks it's silly to cry over a spilled snack.

But I tell him it's not silly when someone feels sad.

FRIENDSHIP GROWS!

We cheer our classmate up by offering her some of our popcorn.

I can be a good friend by listening when Nihal says he's afraid of snakes.

He doesn't want anyone else to know, so I won't say anything.

FRIENDSHIP GROWS!

Nihal feels relieved and says, "Thank you!"

I can be a good friend by making sure everyone in my class knows it's time for the group photo. We all need to be in it!

FRIENDSHIP GROWS!

We do a big group high five after the picture!

My teacher was right!

When we're good friends to one another, our friendships grow stronger.

From now on, I'm going to try very hard to be a good friend to everyone.

Because that makes everybody feel great!

WHAT MAKES A GOOD FRIEND?

Everyone enjoys playing with their friends. But did you know being a good friend means a lot more than just having fun? There are so many different ways to be a good friend every day!

Each of the boxes below describes one way in which a good friend may behave. Read the words and examples from the story together with a grown-up. Then come up with examples of how you've been a good friend!

PATIENT:

This means not getting upset when something takes a long time.

Example: Hikaru waits for Nihal to get off the bus.

HELPFUL:

This means making it easier for someone else to do something.

Example: Hikaru helps Nihal finish his checklist.

LOYAL:
This means being true to your friends.

Example: Hikaru keeps his promise to eat lunch with Nihal.

SHARING:
This means using something together with another person.

Example: Hikaru shares his seat with Nihal.

CONSIDERATE:
This means thinking about other people's feelings.

Example: Hikaru listens when Nihal says he's afraid of snakes.

COOPERATIVE:
This means working together.

Example: Hikaru and Nihal work together to find the animals on the zoo map.

COMPASSIONATE:
This means feeling bad for someone who is sad or hurt.

Example: Hikaru doesn't laugh at the child who is crying.

When was a time when you were patient, helpful, loyal, a good sharer, considerate, compassionate, or cooperative?

ZOO MAP

LET'S BE A GOOD FRIEND

How would you choose to be a good friend in each of the examples that follow?

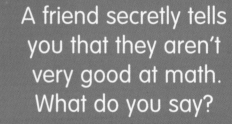

A friend secretly tells you that they aren't very good at math. What do you say?

A classmate falls and scrapes their knee on the playground. What do you do?

A classmate dares you to throw a dodgeball at another child on the playground because "no one likes them." What do you do?

You promised to go to one friend's birthday party, but then you get an invitation to a second party on the same day. What do you do?

BIRTHDAY PARTY MAMO 9/23

BIRTHDAY PARTY ALEX 9/23

Your classmate forgot their markers at home, but you have yours. What do you do?

GLOSSARY

compassionate (kuhm-PASH-uhn-it) feeling sympathy for and a desire to help someone who is suffering
   Luke was compassionate when he hugged the little girl who was crying.

considerate (kuhn-SID-ur-it) careful and concerned for other people's needs and feelings
   Molly is always considerate of her classmate's feelings.

cooperative (koh-AH-pur-uh-tiv) willing to work together toward the same goal
   It's important to be cooperative when you're working as a team.

helpful (HELP-fuhl) willing to make it possible or easier for another person to do something
   Mary felt helpful when she passed out papers for the teacher.

loyal (LOI-uhl) being faithful to one's family, friends, or beliefs

Louise was a loyal teammate who wore her soccer uniform with pride.

patient (PAY-shuhnt) able to put up with problems and delays without getting angry or upset

The teacher was patient as her students completed the activity.

promised (PRAH-mist) when someone has pledged that they will do something

Sue promised her mom she would keep her room clean.

sharing (SHAIR-ing) the act of using something together

My friend forgot her snack, so I didn't mind sharing my grapes.

ABOUT THE AUTHOR

Meredith Rusu has written more than 100 children's books. She lives in New Jersey with her husband and two young sons whom she tries (very hard!) to remind to be kind every day.

ABOUT THE ILLUSTRATOR

Alexandra Colombo has illustrated more than 100 books that have been published all over the world. She loves walking in the woods, writing poetry, and discovering new places. She lives in Italy with her turtle, Carlo, and her dog, Ary.